DREAM TEAM
1996 SCRAPBOOK

Joe Layden

SCHOLASTIC INC.

New York Toronto London Auckland Sydney

To Sue and Emily — my dream team.
—J.L.

Photo Credits
Cover, 4, 27 (bottom), Poster: NBA Photo Library. **3, 7 (both), 8, 9 (action), 11 (action), 13 (action), 14, 15 (both), 19 (both), 21 (action), 23 (both), 25 (action):** NBA/Nathaniel S. Butler. **5, 9 (still), 11 (still), 13 (still), 17 (both), 21 (still), 22, 25 (still), 26, 27 (top):** NBA/Andrew D. Bernstein. **6, 12, 16:** NBA/Barry Gossage. **10:** NBA/Norm Perdue. **18, 30 (Azzi), 31 (Swoopes):** NBA/Scott Cunningham. **20:** NBA/Andy Hayt. **24:** NBA/Bill Baptist. **28, 29, 30 (McClain):** NBA/Steven Freeman. **30 (Bolton/Lobo/Leslie/Edwards), 31 (Steding/McGhee):** NBA/ Lou Capozzola. **31 (McCray/Staley):** NBA/Noren Trotman.

USOC Official Licensed Product 36USC380

ISBN 0-590-89661-X

© 1996 NBA Properties, Inc.
© 1996 USA Basketball, Inc.
All rights reserved. Published by Scholastic Inc.

12 11 10 9 8 7 6 5 4 3 2 1   6 7 8 9/9 0 1/0

A DREAM COME TRUE

From the streets of New York to the farms of Indiana to the mountains of Kentucky, basketball is a wildly popular game in the United States. It is played on asphalt, concrete, hardwood, or dirt. But nowhere is its simple beauty more evident than in the National Basketball Association (NBA), home of the greatest players on the planet.

At the 1996 Olympic Games in Atlanta, Georgia, the hopes of the United States will once again be riding on the sturdy shoulders of the NBA's finest athletes.

Coached by Lenny Wilkens, the 1996 U.S. Olympic Dream Team is an explosive collection of talent with the potential to equal the awesome accomplishments of its predecessors. It is a team without a noticeable weakness; a team that will unite in Atlanta this summer for one mission: to keep the dream alive!

DREAM TEAM 1996 ROSTER*

No.	Name	Pos.	Ht.	Wt.	Birth Date	NBA Team
6	Anfernee Hardaway	Guard	6'7"	215	7/8/72	Orlando Magic
5	Grant Hill	Forward	6'8"	225	10/5/72	Detroit Pistons
11	Karl Malone	Forward	6'9"	256	7/24/63	Utah Jazz
10	Reggie Miller	Guard	6'7"	185	8/24/65	Indiana Pacers
15	Hakeem Olajuwon	Center	7'0"	255	1/21/63	Houston Rockets
13	Shaquille O'Neal	Center	7'1"	301	3/6/72	Orlando Magic
8	Scottie Pippen	Forward	6'7"	225	9/25/65	Chicago Bulls
7	David Robinson	Center	7'1"	250	8/6/65	San Antonio Spurs
14	Glenn Robinson	Forward	6'7"	240	1/10/73	Milwaukee Bucks
12	John Stockton	Guard	6'1"	175	3/26/62	Utah Jazz

Head Coach: Lenny Wilkens, Atlanta Hawks
Assistant Coaches: Bobby Cremins, Georgia Tech; Clem Haskins, University of Minnesota; Jerry Sloan, Utah Jazz

* Two players will be added after publication of this book.

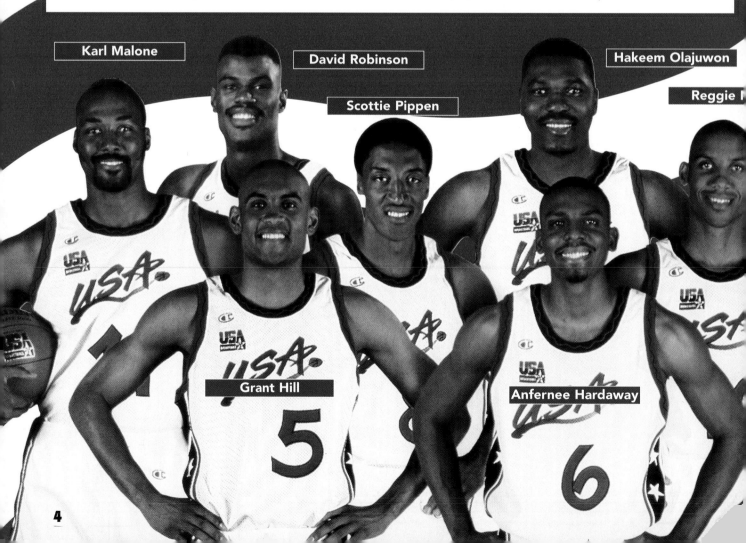

Karl Malone

David Robinson

Scottie Pippen

Hakeem Olajuwon

Reggie [Miller]

Grant Hill

Anfernee Hardaway

"IT'S A TREMENDOUS HONOR to coach the United States Olympic basketball team. I was very proud to be a part of the 1992 squad and I look forward to being the head coach of the 1996 team."

Lenny Wilkens

Shaquille O'Neal

Glenn Robinson

John Stockton

At a glance, it might seem like coaching the United States Olympic men's basketball team would be an easy job. After all, with this much talent, all you have to do is roll out the ball, sit back, and enjoy the show. Right?

Not exactly. The man who leads the Dream Team into Atlanta for the 1996 Olympic Games must be a skilled tactician, manager, and motivator. Not only will he be expected to make the proper substitutions and call the right plays, he'll also have to soothe an occasional bruised ego. With this many superstars on one team, there simply isn't enough playing time to go around.

Fortunately, Dream Team head coach Lenny Wilkens is ideally suited to the job. A member of the Basketball Hall of Fame, Wilkens was named NBA Coach of the Year in 1994, when he led the Atlanta Hawks to the Eastern Conference Semifinals. He is also the winningest coach in NBA history. Perhaps most important, though, Wilkens knows what it's like to be an Olympic coach, having assisted Chuck Daly with the original Dream Team during the 1992 Olympic Games.

ANFERNEE HARDAWAY
"THE MAGIC TOUCH"

"I CAN'T IMAGINE

putting a gold medal around my neck, but if that day comes, I'll be the proudest basketball player in the world."

Anfernee "Penny" Hardaway is one of the most exciting players in the NBA. With his extraordinary combination of passing, scoring, rebounding, and ballhandling skills, he often reminds people of the great Magic Johnson. Even though Penny has been in the league only three seasons, he's been electrifying crowds for years — first as a high school star in Memphis, Tennessee, and then as a college All-American at Memphis State. On NBA Draft Day 1993, when Orlando traded number-one pick Chris Webber to Golden State in exchange for Penny and three future first-round picks, some Magic fans were unhappy. It wasn't long, however, before they realized this Penny was worth his weight in gold.

Career Highlights

- National High School Player of the Year (1990)
- First-Team NCAA All-America (1992–93)
- Named to NBA All-Rookie First Team (1993–94)

Did you know...

When Anfernee Hardaway was a little boy, his grandmother used to say he was "Pretty as a penny." Pretty soon, his friends started calling him "Penny." The nickname stuck, and Anfernee has been answering to Penny ever since.

CAREER STATISTICS

GP	FG%	FT%	Rebounds	Assists	Points	Avg.
159	.490	.758	775	1,095	2,926	18.4

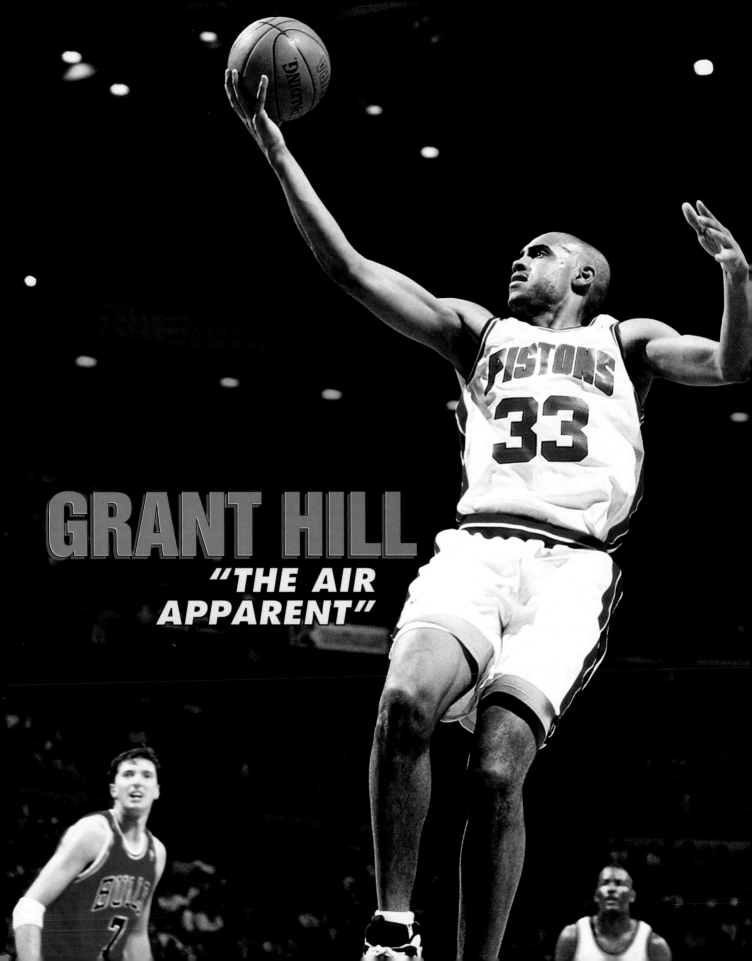

GRANT HILL

"THE AIR APPARENT"

C A R E E R   S T A T I S T I C S

GP	FG%	FT%	Rebounds	Assists	Points	Avg.
70	.477	.732	445	353	1,394	19.9

"EVERY TIME I THINK TO MYSELF

that I'm on the Olympic team, I feel like a little kid."

It's not easy being compared to the greatest player in basketball history. But Grant Hill is accustomed to high expectations. After all, his father, Calvin Hill, was an All-Pro running back with the Dallas Cowboys and Washington Redskins. So when Grant first heard his name mentioned in the same breath as Michael Jordan's, he simply shrugged it off. Of course, Grant has done nothing to discourage the notion that he's one of the best players to come along in some time. Since joining the Detroit Pistons, Grant has emerged as an exceptional all-around player, as well as a first-class individual. It's no surprise, then, that Grant is a favorite with NBA fans.

Career Highlights

- Won two NCAA titles at Duke University (1991, 1992)
- Co-NBA Rookie of the Year in 1995
- Leading vote-getter for 1995 and 1996 NBA All-Star Games

Did you know...

In 1995, *People* magazine included Grant on its list of the "50 most beautiful people in the world."

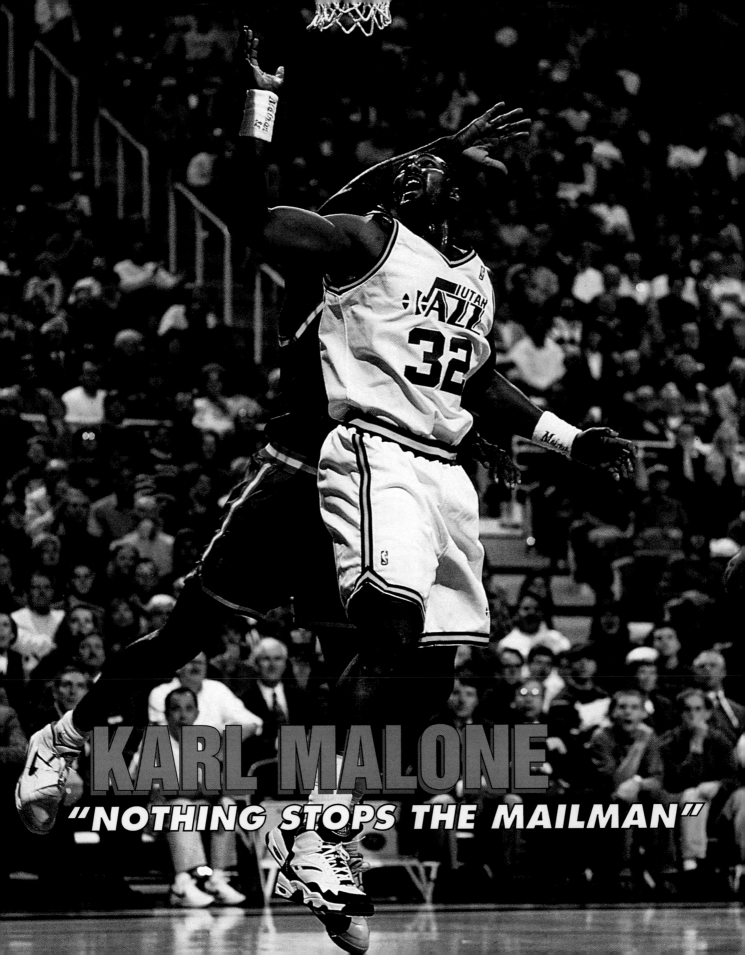

KARL MALONE
"NOTHING STOPS THE MAILMAN"

"ANY TIME YOU HAVE THE OPPORTUNITY

to represent your country, it's an honor."

GP	FG%	FT%	Rebounds	Assists	Points	Avg.
816	.526	.721	8,929	2,470	21,237	26.0

When Karl Malone was a college star at Louisiana Tech, he acquired the nickname "The Mailman" because of his ability to deliver. In his decade-long career with the Utah Jazz, Karl has done nothing to change anybody's mind. Night in and night out, The Mailman continues to deliver the goods. At 6'9", 256 pounds, Karl is among the strongest forwards in the NBA. He uses that muscle to overpower opponents under the boards. In addition, Karl can often be found on the wing, taking a neat no-look pass from teammate John Stockton, and then soaring down the lane for an easy layup.

Did you know...

Karl is one of the most durable players in NBA history. A true iron man, he missed only four regular-season games in his first 10 years in the league.

Career Highlights

- MVP of NBA All-Star Game (1989, 1993)
- Member of U.S. Olympic Dream Team in 1992 and 1996
- Utah Jazz' all-time leader in points and rebounds

REGGIE MILLER
"STRAIGHT SHOOTER"

"PLAYING FOR YOUR COUNTRY *has to be right up there with winning the NBA championship. It's an awesome feeling."*

CAREER STATISTICS

GP	FG%	FT%	Rebounds	Assists	Points	Avg.
644	.493	.879	2,056	2,067	12,467	19.4

Career Highlights

- Indiana Pacers' all-time scoring leader
- Selected to the 1994 Dream Team and 1996 Dream Team
- Led NBA in free-throw percentage (.918) in 1994–95

Reggie Miller is one of the best outside shooters in the NBA. But what really distinguishes the Indiana Pacers' 6' 7", 190-pound guard is his attitude. When the game is on the line, Reggie wants the ball in his hands. Brash, outspoken, and surprisingly confident, he thrives on pressure. That's why many of Reggie's greatest performances have come in front of loud, vocal crowds. In the 1994 NBA Playoffs, for example, he put on a remarkable offensive display, scoring 25 points in the fourth quarter of a game against the New York Knicks at Madison Square Garden.

Did you know...

Reggie's older sister, Cheryl, was an All-American basketball player who helped lead the United States to a gold medal at the 1984 Olympic Games?

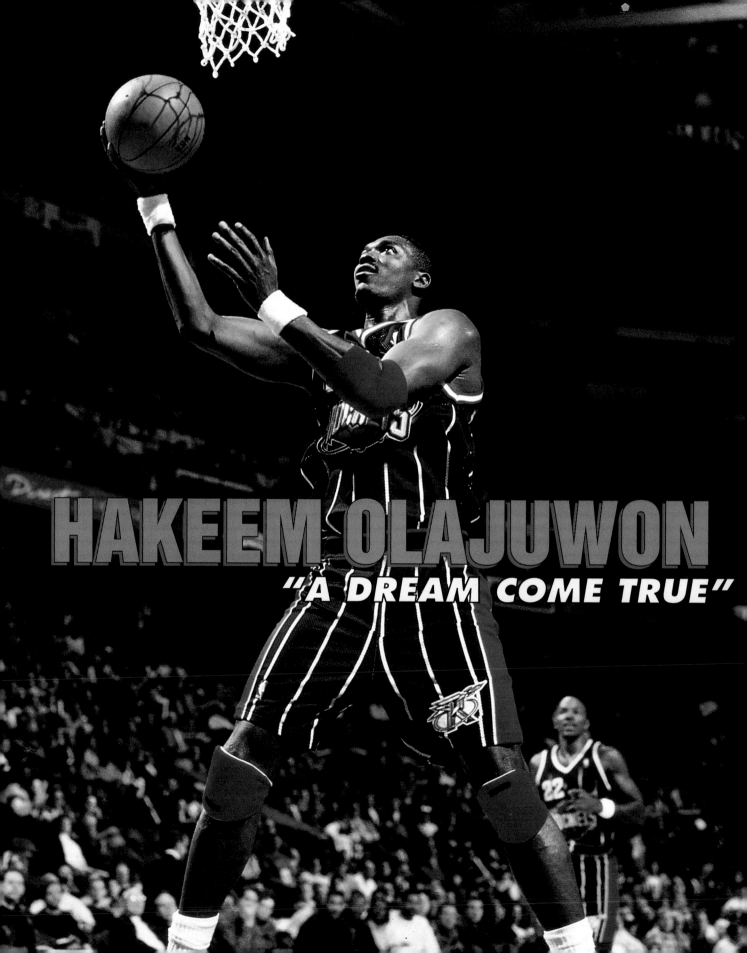

HAKEEM OLAJUWON
"A DREAM COME TRUE"

"I STILL CAN'T BELIEVE IT—

it's still like a dream. You cannot ask for anything more."

Career Highlights

- Named NBA Most Valuable Player in 1994
- Voted MVP of NBA Finals in 1994 and 1995
- Five-time All-NBA First Team

Somehow, Hakeem "The Dream" Olajuwon defies the aging process. With each passing season his game becomes sharper, more refined. Even after 12 years in the NBA, there are no visible signs of weakness in his body or spirit. The 7'0", 250-pound center from Lagos, Nigeria, who became a U.S. citizen in 1993, is one of the most talented pivotmen in league history, capable of dominating a game at either end of the floor. A devout Muslim, Hakeem is a fierce competitor, but gracious in both victory and defeat. As his two NBA championship rings attest, though, there have been far more wins than losses.

Did you know...

Hakeem did not start playing basketball until he was 15 years old. He was introduced to the game at a Nigerian sports festival, where he was playing soccer and team handball.

CAREER STATISTICS

GP	FG%	FT%	Rebounds	Assists	Points	Avg.
828	.516	.710	10,239	2,135	19,904	24.0

SHAQUILLE O'NEAL
"THE SHAQ ATTACK"

**Pullout
Poster**

GLENN ROBINSON   KARL MALONE   SCOTTIE PIPPEN

DAVID ROBINSON   JOHN STOCKTON

TEAM™

ANFERNEE HARDAWAY

GRANT HILL

EEM OLAJUWON

SHAQUILLE O'NEAL

REGGIE MILLER

**Pullout
Poster**

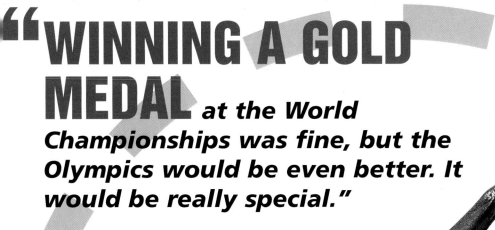

"WINNING A GOLD MEDAL *at the World Championships was fine, but the Olympics would be even better. It would be really special."*

Did you know...

Shaq was seven feet tall by the time he was a senior in high school. In two years at Robert Cole High in San Antonio, Texas, his varsity team won 68 games and lost just once.

Shaquille O'Neal is more than just an athlete. He is an industry: movie star, rap singer, walking billboard. But it's basketball that makes Shaq what he is. As the imposing center for the Orlando Magic, O'Neal rivals Disney World as one of Florida's top tourist attractions. Though he has been in the NBA for only four years, Shaq is already being compared to the greatest centers in NBA history. And why not? With his ability to rebound, block shots, and run the floor, Shaq might be the most dominant player in the game.

Career Highlights

- No. 1 pick in 1992 NBA Draft
- NBA Rookie of the Year in 1993
- MVP 1994 World Championship of Basketball

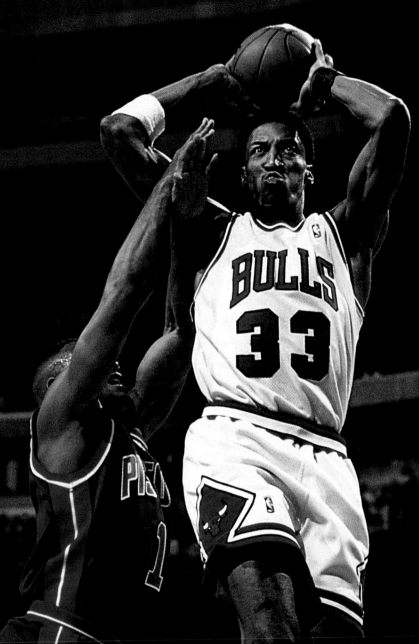

SCOTTIE PIPPEN
"STEPPING OUT OF THE SHADOWS"

"WE ARE THE BEST
basketball team in the world, and we should never lose."

CAREER STATISTICS

GP	FG%	FT%	Rebounds	Assists	Points	Avg.
630	.489	.688	3,940	3,271	10,994	17.5

Did you know...

Although Scottie has played his entire professional career with the Chicago Bulls, he was actually selected by the Seattle SuperSonics in the 1987 NBA Draft. He was traded to the Bulls in a draft-day deal.

When Michael Jordan announced his temporary retirement from basketball in 1993, most people expected the Chicago Bulls to plummet from the top of the NBA heap. Thanks primarily to Scottie Pippen, though, they remained one of the league's best teams. Scottie led the Bulls to an impressive 55-win season in Jordan's absence and emerged as a superstar in his own right. Scottie is a gifted and versatile player, capable of posting up under the basket or running the offense from the point. And whether he's chasing a guard or banging against a center in the paint, Scottie is also one of the best defenders in the NBA.

Career Highlights

- Member of three NBA championship teams (1991, 1992, 1993)
- Won Olympic gold medal in 1992
- Named to All-NBA First Team in 1994 and 1995

DAVID ROBINSON
"AN OFFICER AND A GENTLEMAN"

"TO WIN THE NBA CHAMPIONSHIP

is probably the top goal of most players. But a gold medal? How can you say that's not right at the top, too?"

CAREER STATISTICS

GP	FG%	FT%	Rebounds	Assists	Points	Avg.
475	.527	.744	5,921	1,471	12,209	25.7

David Robinson is one of the finest centers in the game of basketball. Lean and muscular, with a soft shooting touch and a quick first step to the basket, he is a versatile athlete with no real shortcomings. But there is more than merely basketball to David Robinson. "The Admiral" is also respected for his intelligence and dignity. A 1987 graduate of the U.S. Naval Academy, David served two years in the military before embarking on his NBA career. He is a quiet and deeply religious man who likes to spend time with his family.

Did you know...

David is a talented musician who plays both the saxophone and piano. He brings a keyboard on the road and often relaxes by composing songs.

Career Highlights

- No. 1 pick in 1987 NBA Draft
- Member of U.S. Olympic team in 1988, 1992, and 1996
- Named NBA Most Valuable Player in 1995

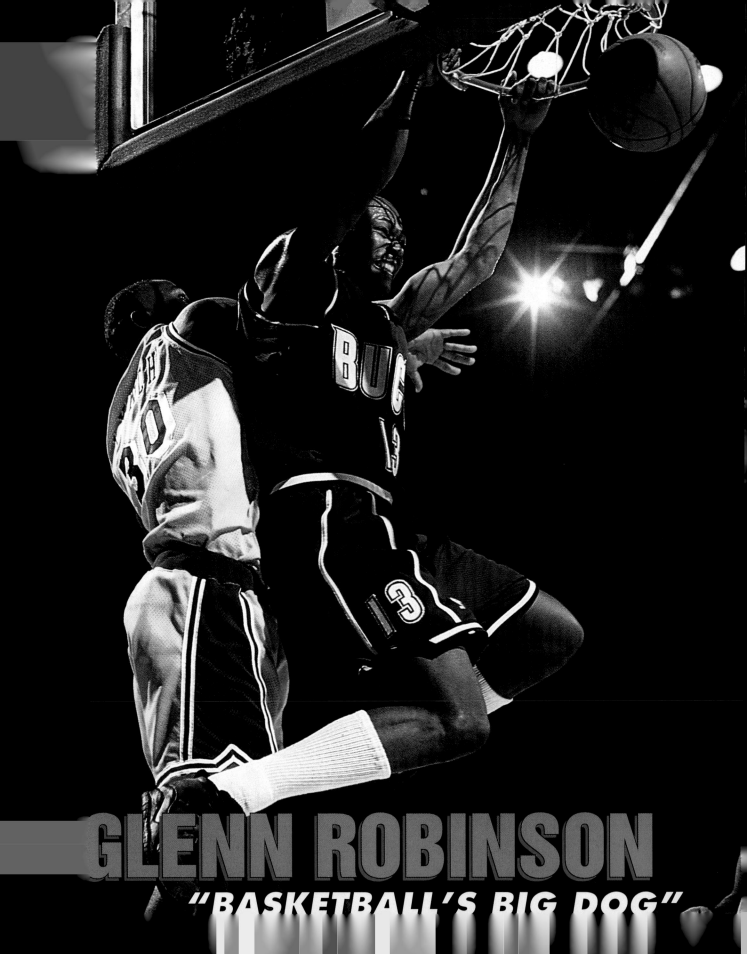

GLENN ROBINSON
"BASKETBALL'S BIG DOG"

"ONLY SPECIAL PLAYERS

who have been in this league have had a chance to put that Olympic medal around their necks."

CAREER STATISTICS

GP	FG%	FT%	Rebounds	Assists	Points	Avg.
80	.451	.796	513	197	1,755	21.9

When the Milwaukee Bucks won the NBA Draft Lottery in 1994, they had no doubts about the player who would best fit their program. They believed the best player in college basketball that year was Glenn Robinson, a 6'7" power forward from Purdue University. Known affectionately as "Big Dog," Glenn was a magnificent offensive player. After averaging more than 30 points per game as a junior, it was obvious that he was ready for the NBA. Expectations were high for Glenn, and he did not disappoint. The "Big Dog" will be a major force for years to come.

Career Highlights

- College Player of the Year in 1994
- NCAA scoring champion in 1993–94
- No. 1 pick in 1994 NBA Draft

Did you know...

Glenn led all NBA rookies in scoring in 1994–95 with an average of 21.9 points per game. He was the first Milwaukee player in more than a decade to finish among the NBA's top 10 scorers.

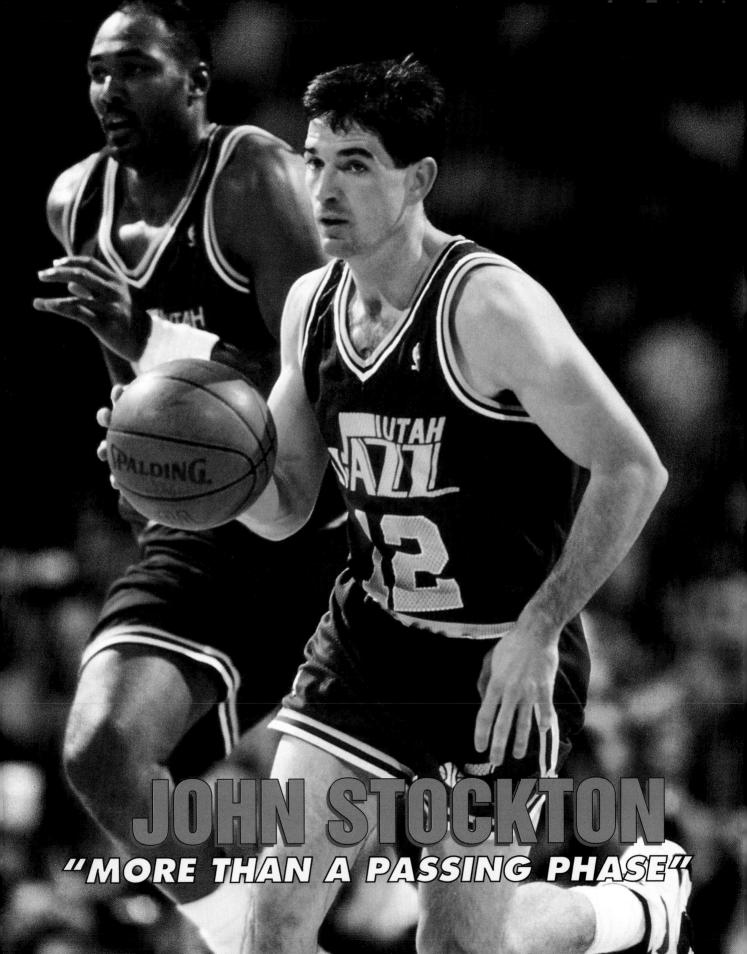

JOHN STOCKTON
"MORE THAN A PASSING PHASE"

CAREER STATISTICS

GP	FG%	FT%	Rebounds	Assists	Points	Avg.
898	.515	.820	2,379	10,394	12,076	13.4

"PUTTING ON THE UNITED STATES' UNIFORM

is something I've dreamt about since I was a little kid."

Career Highlights

- Named All-NBA First Team in 1994 and 1995
- All-time NBA leader in assists
- Won Olympic gold medal in 1992

At 6'1", 175 pounds, point guard John Stockton is one of the smaller players in the NBA. But he's also one of the most durable. For 12 years he has been running the offense for the Utah Jazz, and he's done the job about as well as it's ever been done. Blessed with remarkable court sense and vision, as well as exceptional ballhandling and passing ability, John is the NBA's all-time leader in assists. As long as John is in the middle on a fast break, with the ball in his hands, it's good news for the Jazz. And bad news for the defense.

Did you know...

While the vast majority of NBA players in recent years have switched to long, baggy shorts, John prefers the shorter, traditional cut. In fact, his uniform has to be specially tailored!

HOW THE DREAM BEGAN...

The 1992 United States Olympic men's basketball team was assembled with one goal in mind: to bring home the gold medal. Nothing less would be acceptable. For the first time, professional basketball players from the United States would be competing in the Olympic Games. And, as everyone knew, the best basketball in the world was played in the NBA.

The original U.S. Olympic Dream Team included some of the greatest players the game has ever known, including Michael Jordan, Larry Bird, and Magic Johnson. It was a collection of superstars, all of whom understood that individual statistics and accomplishments meant nothing if they came back from Barcelona, Spain, without a Gold Medal.

In the end, there was little reason for concern. The Dream Team was the hit of the 1992 Olympic Games, winning by an average of nearly 44 points per game and thrilling audiences from all over the world. So mesmerizing were the members of the Dream Team that even their opponents often stopped to applaud and ask for autographs.

DREAM TEAM 1992 RECORD

USA 116, Angola 48
USA 103, Croatia 70
USA 111, Germany 68
USA 127, Brazil 83
USA 122, Spain 81
USA 115, Puerto Rico 77
USA 127, Lithuania 76
USA 117, Croatia 85

DREAM TEAM 1994 RECORD

USA 115, Spain 100
USA 132, China 77
USA 105, Brazil 82
USA 130, Australia 74
USA 134, Puerto Rico 83
USA 111, Russia 94
USA 97, Greece 58
USA 137, Russia 91

The second Dream Team featured a younger group of players out to make a name for themselves. At the 1994 World Championship of Basketball in Toronto, Canada, the Dream Team upheld the tradition established by its predecessor by capturing the gold medal with a perfect record.

Michael Jordan ▶

The Original Dream Team

◀

DREAM TEAM 1992 STATS

Name	Points/Avg.	REB/Avg.	Assists
Charles Barkley	144/18.0	33/4.1	19
Larry Bird	67/8.4	30/3.8	14
Clyde Drexler	84/10.5	24/3.0	29
Patrick Ewing	76/9.5	42/5.3	3
Magic Johnson	48/8.0	14/2.3	33
Michael Jordan	119/14.9	19/2.4	38
Christian Laettner	38/4.8	20/2.5	3
Karl Malone	104/13.0	42/5.3	9
Chris Mullin	103/12.9	13/1.6	29
Scottie Pippen	72/9.0	17/2.1	47
David Robinson	72/9.0	33/4.1	7
John Stockton	11/2.8	1/0.3	8

The 1994 Dream Team

▶

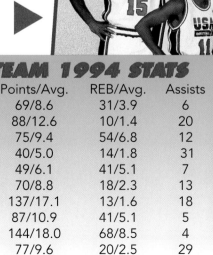

DREAM TEAM 1994 STATS

Name	Points/Avg.	REB/Avg.	Assists
Derrick Coleman	69/8.6	31/3.9	6
Joe Dumars	88/12.6	10/1.4	20
Shawn Kemp	75/9.4	54/6.8	12
Kevin Johnson	40/5.0	14/1.8	31
Larry Johnson	49/6.1	41/5.1	7
Dan Majerle	70/8.8	18/2.3	13
Reggie Miller	137/17.1	13/1.6	18
Alonzo Mourning	87/10.9	41/5.1	5
Shaquille O'Neal	144/18.0	68/8.5	4
Mark Price	77/9.6	20/2.5	29
Steve Smith	24/3.0	10/1.3	14
Dominique Wilkins	101/12.6	26/3.3	8

USA BASKETBALL WOMEN'S NATIONAL TEAM

They may not be as famous as their male counterparts, but the players who comprise the USA Basketball Women's National Team have some pretty big dreams of their own. The 11-player squad, which was selected in the spring of 1995, includes such former collegiate stars as Sheryl Swoopes, Teresa Edwards, Dawn Staley, and Rebecca Lobo. This team is expected to form the core of the 1996 U.S. Olympic team which will be named in the spring of 1996. Many of these athletes have strengthened and refined their games by playing professionally in Europe and Japan. Now they have committed one year of their lives to a common goal: to give the United States its first gold medal in Olympic women's basketball since 1988.

Dawn Staley · Teresa Edwards · Katy Steding · Nikki McCray · Jennifer Azzi · Ruthie Bolton

Katrina McClain · Rebecca Lobo · Lisa Leslie · Carla McGhee · Sheryl Swoopes

The Coach

The 1996 U.S. Olympic women's basketball team will be coached by Tara VanDerveer. Like her players, VanDerveer has dedicated herself fully to the task at hand.

VanDerveer's credentials are impeccable. She is one of the most successful collegiate coaches of the past decade. At Stanford she has won two national championships and compiled a career record of 251–62. Coaching an Olympic team, of course, presents an entirely different challenge. But VanDerveer, who has a wealth of international experience, can handle the job.

"I feel it is a tremendous opportunity and a tremendous honor to be named head coach of the 1996 U.S. Olympic team. It'll be a long year with a lot of hard work, but I'm really looking forward to it," says VanDerveer.

USA BASKETBALL WOMEN'S NATIONAL TEAM ROSTER

No.	Name	Pos.	Ht.	Wt.	Birth Date	College
8	Jennifer Azzi	Guard	5'8"	140	8/31/68	Stanford
6	Ruthie Bolton	Guard	5'8"	150	5/25/67	Auburn
4	Teresa Edwards	Guard	5'11"	155	7/19/64	Georgia
9	Lisa Leslie	Fwd/Ctr	6'5"	170	7/7/72	USC
13	Rebecca Lobo	Fwd/Ctr	6'4"	187	10/6/73	Connecticut
12	Katrina McClain	Forward	6'2"	180	9/19/65	Georgia
15	Nikki McCray	Guard	5'11"	158	12/17/71	Tennessee
10	Carla McGhee	Fwd/Ctr	6'2"	165	3/6/68	Tennessee
5	Dawn Staley	Guard	5'6"	125	5/4/70	Virginia
11	Katy Steding	Forward	6'0"	160	12/11/67	Stanford
7	Sheryl Swoopes	Guard	6'0"	145	3/25/71	Texas Tech

Coach: Tara VanDerveer, Stanford University

Jennifer Azzi

Naismith Player of the Year as a senior at Stanford in 1989, when the Cardinals won the NCAA championship; played professionally in Sweden in 1994–95 and averaged 31.6 points per game.

Rebecca Lobo

The youngest member of the team; a versatile center who led Connecticut to the NCAA title in 1995; named College Player of the Year in 1995.

Ruthie Bolton

An excellent outside shooter who hit 52.6 percent of her three-point attempts in the 1994 Goodwill Games.

Teresa Edwards

The first American basketball player to compete in three Olympiads; second-leading scorer on 1988 U.S. Olympic team, which won a gold medal in Seoul, South Korea.

Katrina McClain

A veteran forward who has played professionally in Europe and Asia for the past seven years; named USA Basketball Female Athlete of the Year in 1992; a member of the 1988 and 1992 U.S. Olympic teams.

Lisa Leslie

A strong inside player who led the University of Southern California in scoring and rebounding as a junior and senior; National High School Player of the Year in 1990.

Dawn Staley
A quick guard who led the University of Virginia to three consecutive NCAA Final Four appearances; holds NCAA career record for steals with 454.

Nikki McCray
University of Tennessee guard was Southeastern Conference Player of the Year in 1994 and 1995.

Carla McGhee
A power forward who helped the University of Tennessee win two national titles; has played professionally in Germany, France, and Spain.

Katy Steding
A good long-range shooter; played on Stanford's national championship team in 1990 and set an NCAA record by hitting six three-pointers in a Final Four game.

Sheryl Swoopes
Named 1993 College National Player of the Year; scored 47 points in Texas Tech's 84–82 victory over Ohio State in the 1993 NCAA championship game.

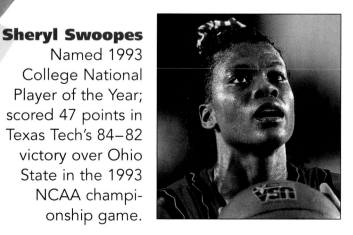

Dream Team QUIZ

1 Which of the following players led the Dream Team in scoring at the 1992 Olympic Games in Barcelona?

A) Charles Barkley
B) Michael Jordan
C) David Robinson

2 Which country did the Dream Team defeat to win the gold medal at the 1992 Olympic Games?

A) Lithuania
B) Spain
C) Croatia

3 Which of the following Dream Team players did not win an NBA Rookie of the Year Award?

A) Magic Johnson
B) Larry Bird
C) Michael Jordan

4 Choose the Dream Team coach who did not play in the NBA:

A) Lenny Wilkens (1996)
B) Don Nelson (1994)
C) Chuck Daly (1992)

5 Which member of the original Dream Team has scored the most points in his career?

A) Michael Jordan
B) Hakeem Olajuwon
C) David Robinson

6 Who is the only player to have earned a spot on a Dream Team roster without having played in an NBA game?

A) Shaquille O'Neal
B) Christian Laettner
C) Shawn Kemp

7 Which member of the 1994 Dream Team won two NBA championships and was named MVP of the NBA Finals?

A) Reggie Miller
B) Joe Dumars
C) Larry Johnson

ANSWERS: 1-A; 2-C; 3-A; 4-C; 5-A; 6-B; 7-B